MODERN DESIGNS
STAINED GLASS
PATTERN BOOK

ANNA CROYLE

DOVER PUBLICATIONS, INC.
MINEOLA, NEW YORK

Copyright

Bibliographical Note

Modern Designs Stained Glass Pattern Book is a new work, first published by Dover Publications, Inc., in 2005.

DOVER *Pictorial Archive* SERIES

International Standard Book Number
ISBN-13: 978-0-486-44662-2
ISBN-10: 0-486-44662-X

Manufactured in the United States of America
Dover Publications, Inc., 31 East 2nd Street, Mineola, N.Y. 11501

PUBLISHER'S NOTE

The term "modern" suggests many qualities, among them simplicity, abstraction, and stylization. Artist Anna Croyle applies these design elements to a wide variety of natural and manmade objects—ranging from a climbing frog, running water, and nautilus shells, to a sailboat, a compass, and cocktail glasses—in this dazzling collection of stained glass patterns. Skillfully blending straight lines, arcs, and other geometric design elements, Croyle offers a fascinating blend of subject matter with ultra-modern framing devices. Some of these imaginative plates contain a single design; others combine several designs in a single plate. The sixty plates in this book, suitable for any number of stained glass projects, may be reproduced in larger or smaller sizes.

This collection of patterns is intended as a supplement to stained glass instruction books (such as *Stained Glass Craft* by J. A. F. Divine and G. Blachford, Dover Publications, Inc., 0-486-22812-6). All materials needed, including general instructions and tools for beginners, can usually be purchased from local craft and hobby stores listed in your Yellow Pages.

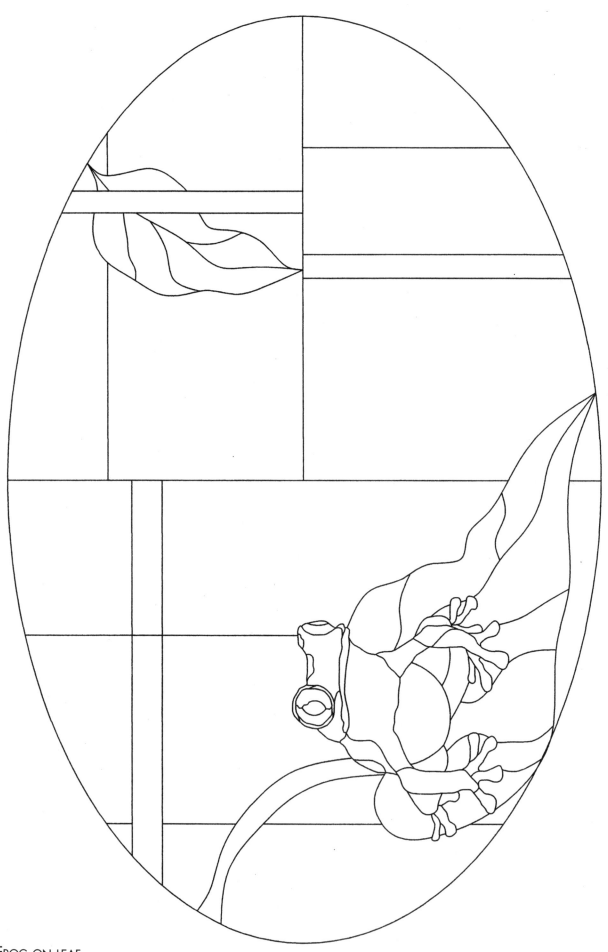

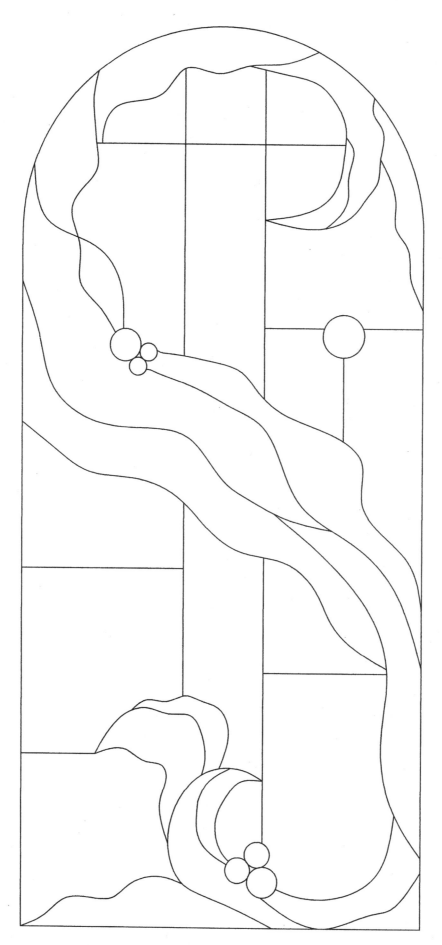

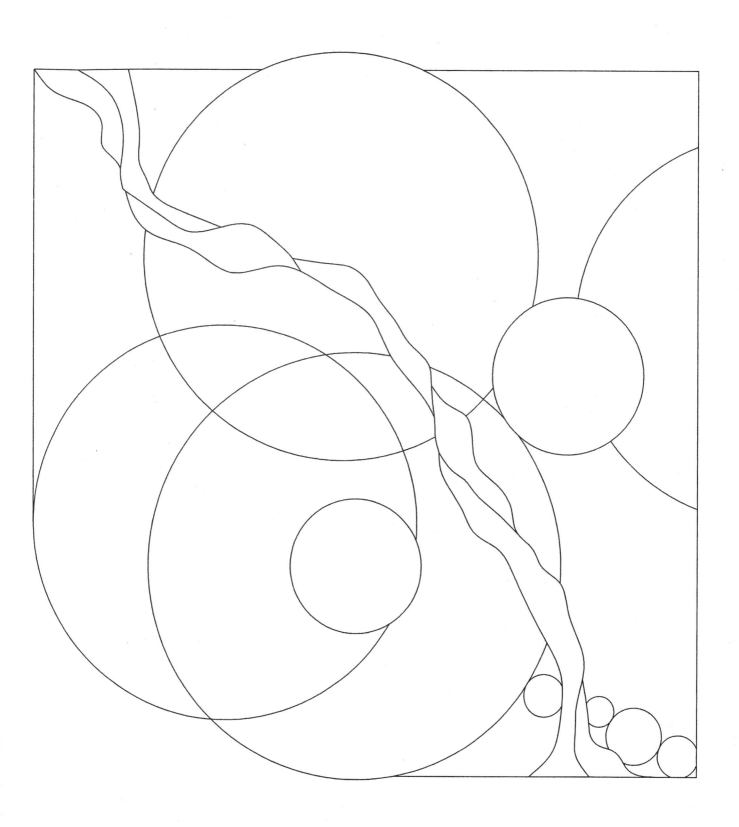

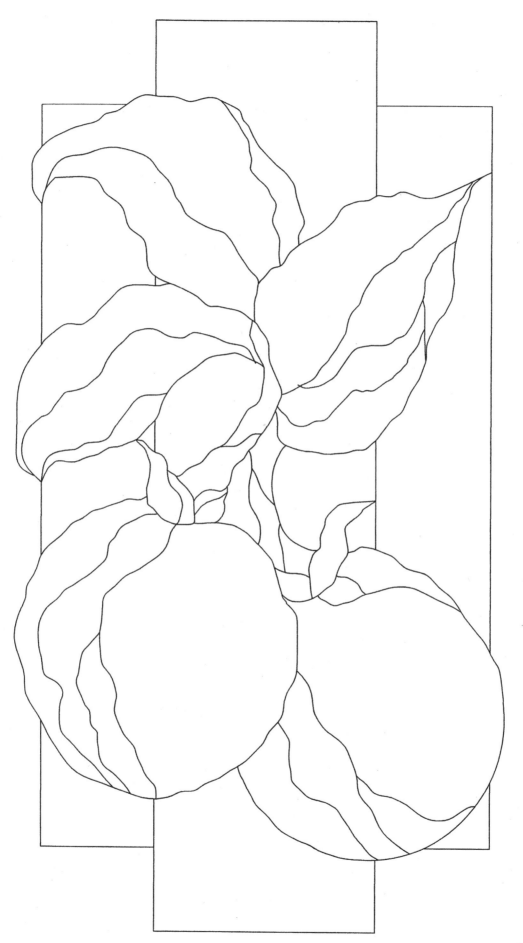

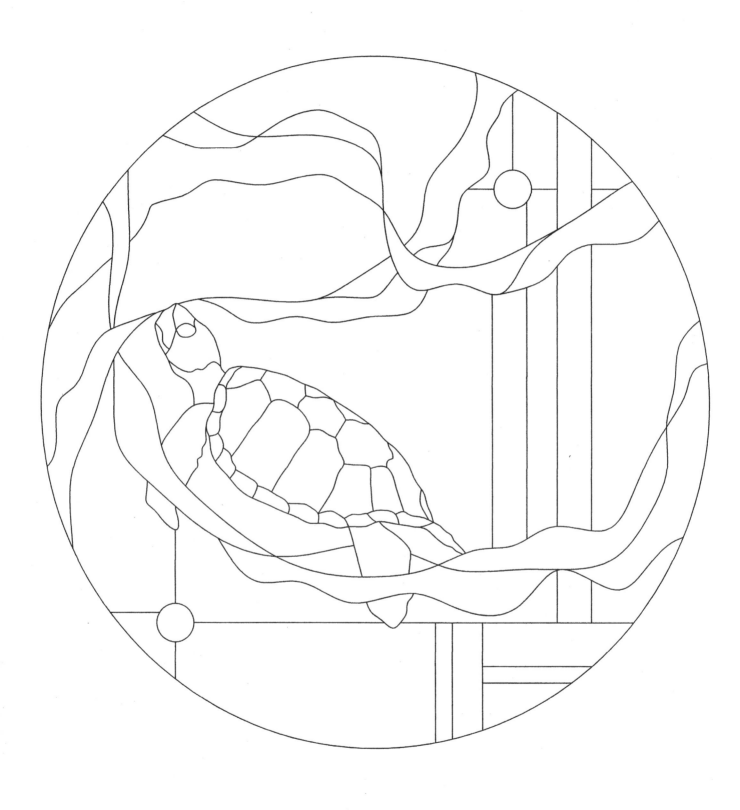

8   SEA TURTLE

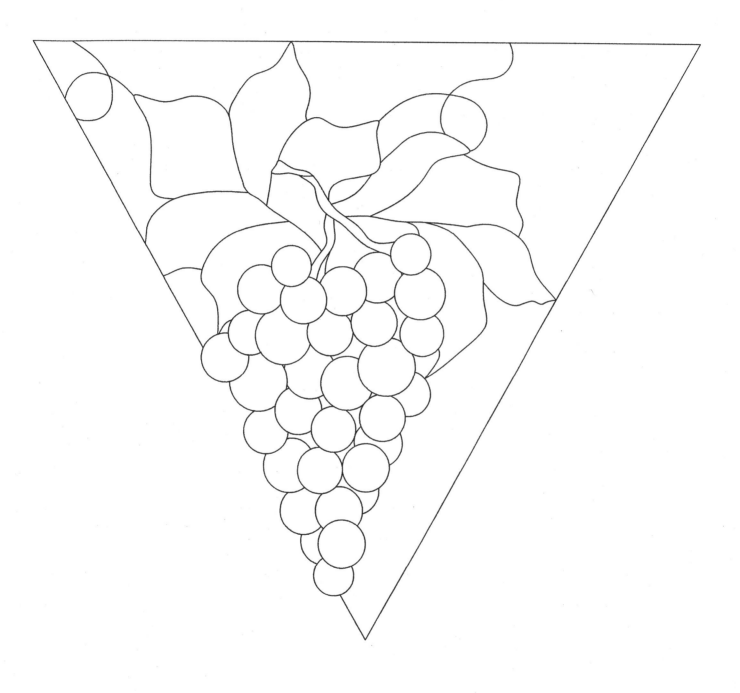

14   Palm tree

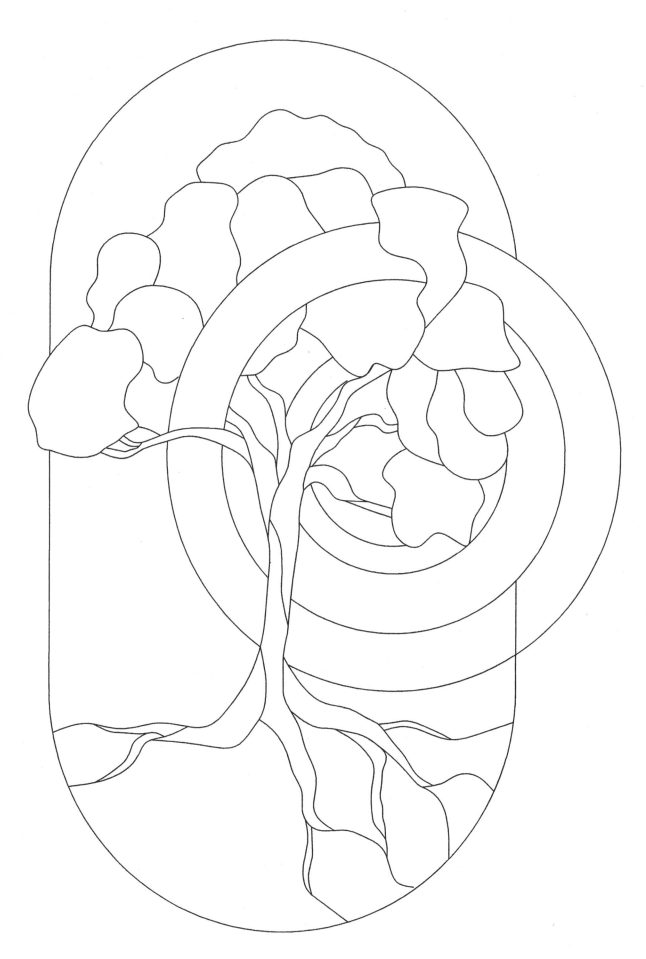

16 LEAFY TREE

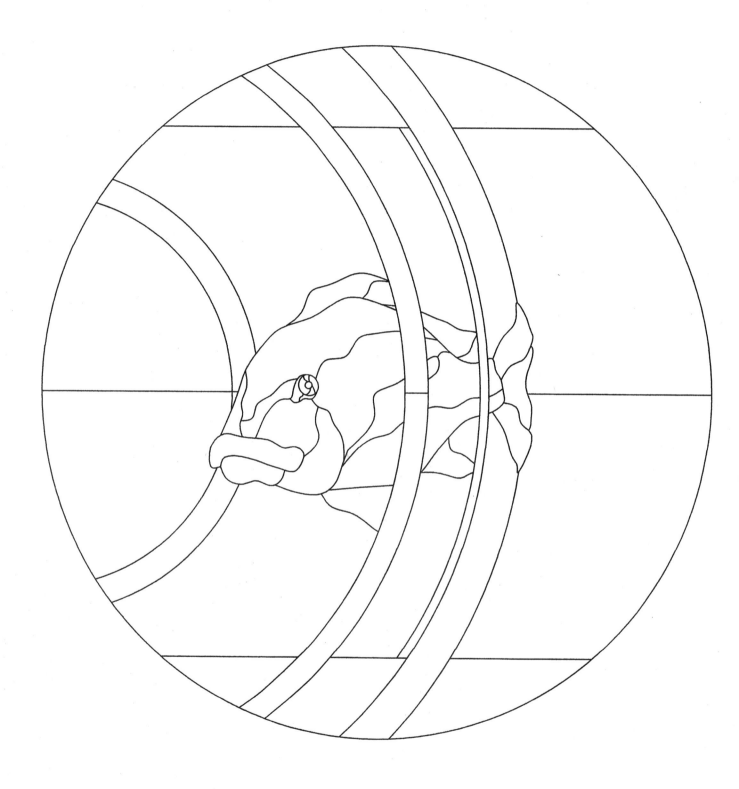

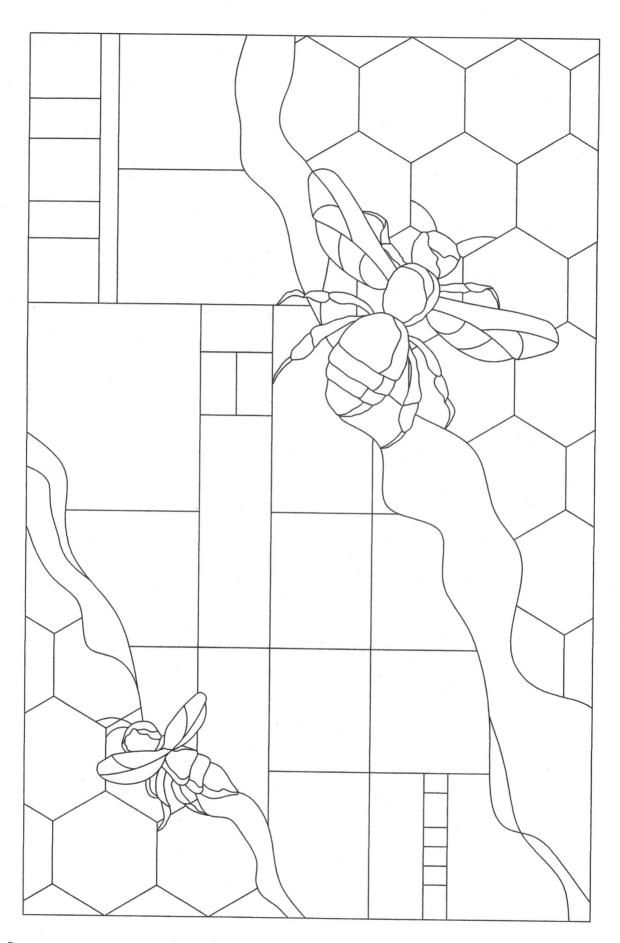

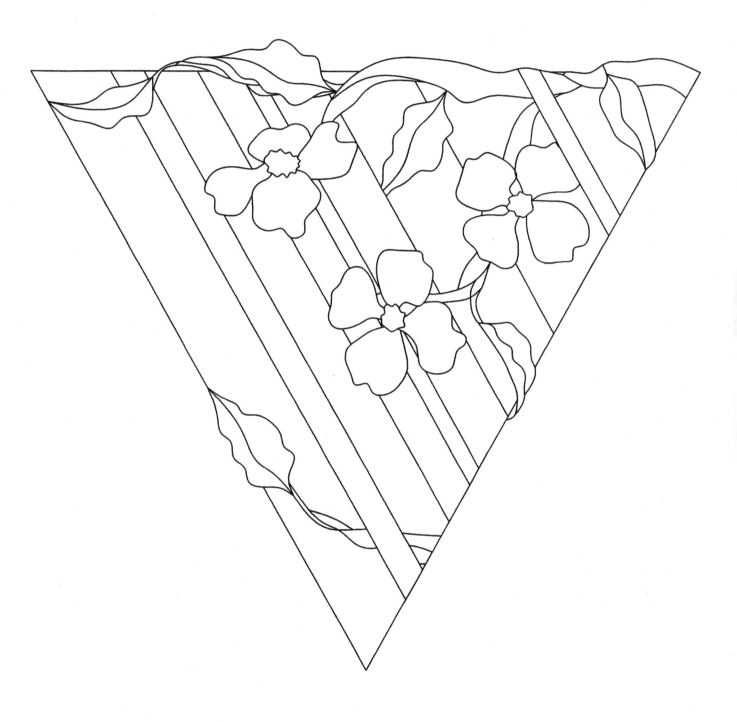

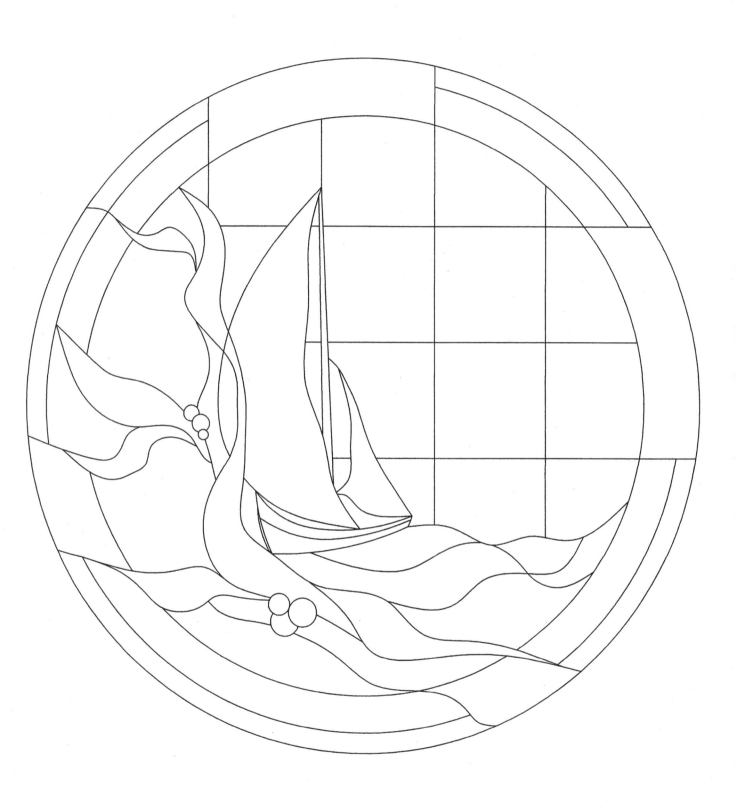

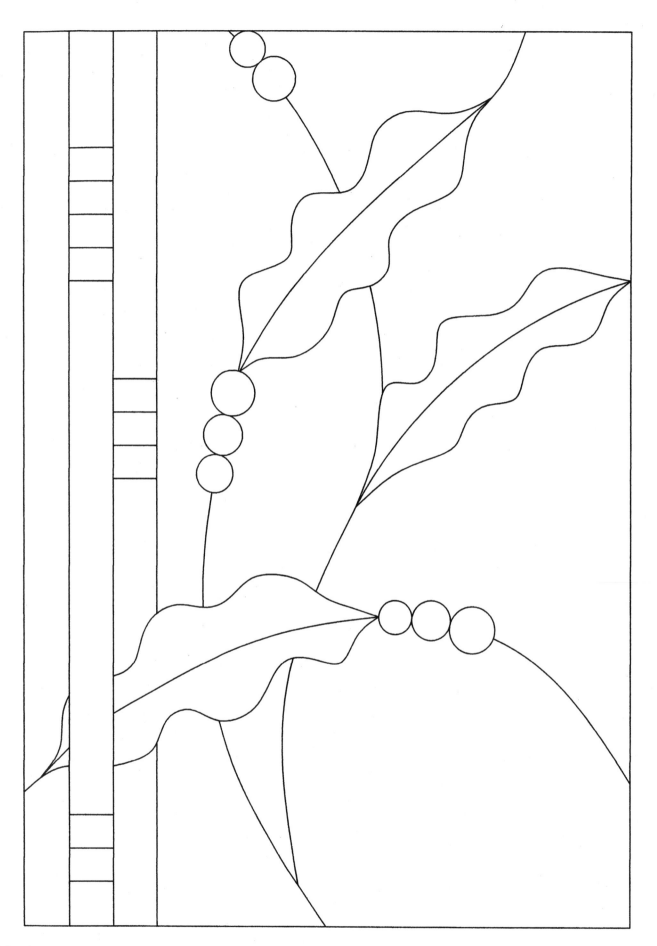

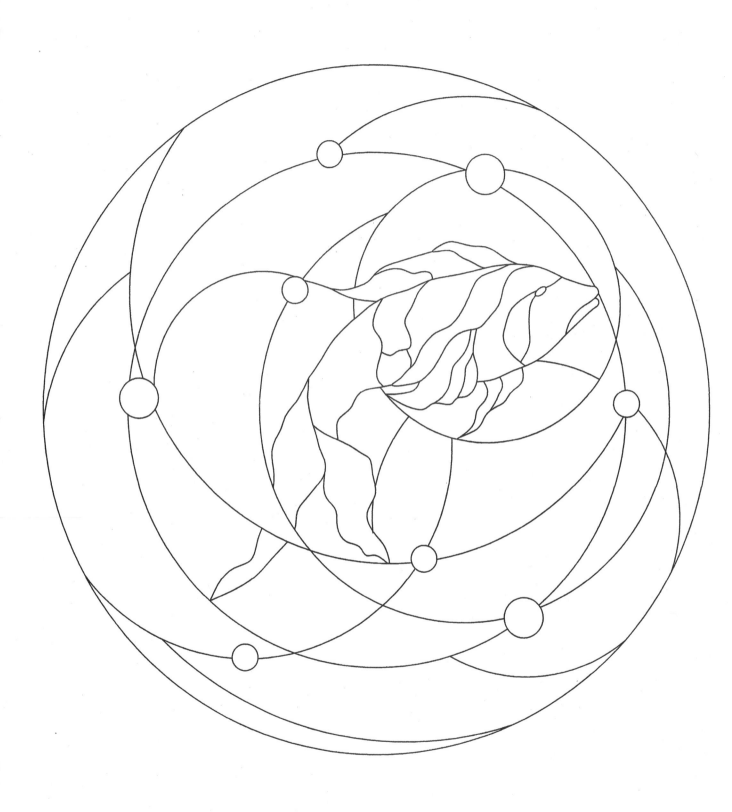

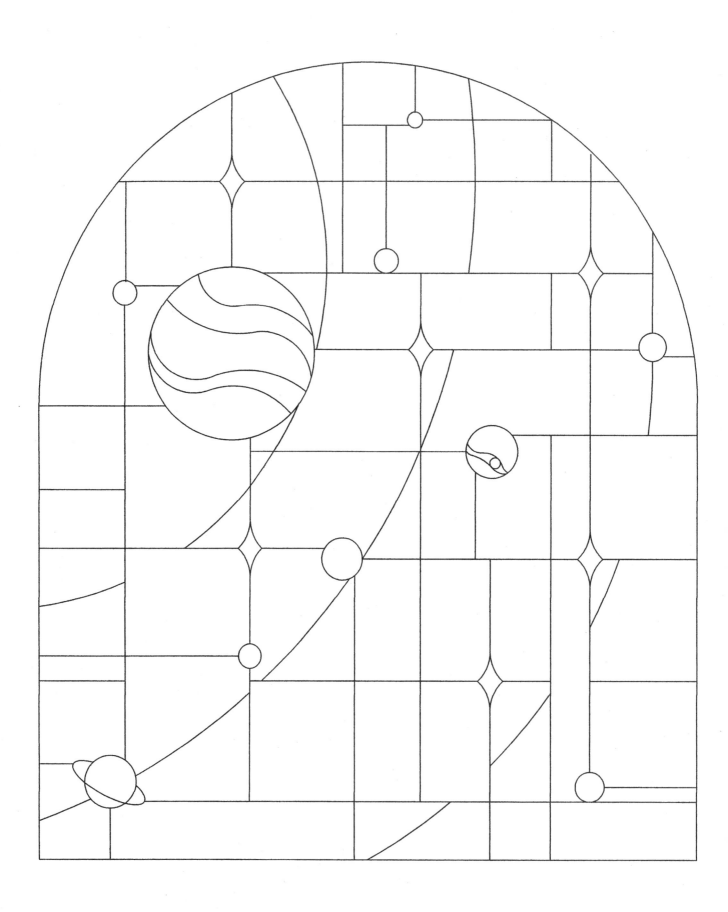

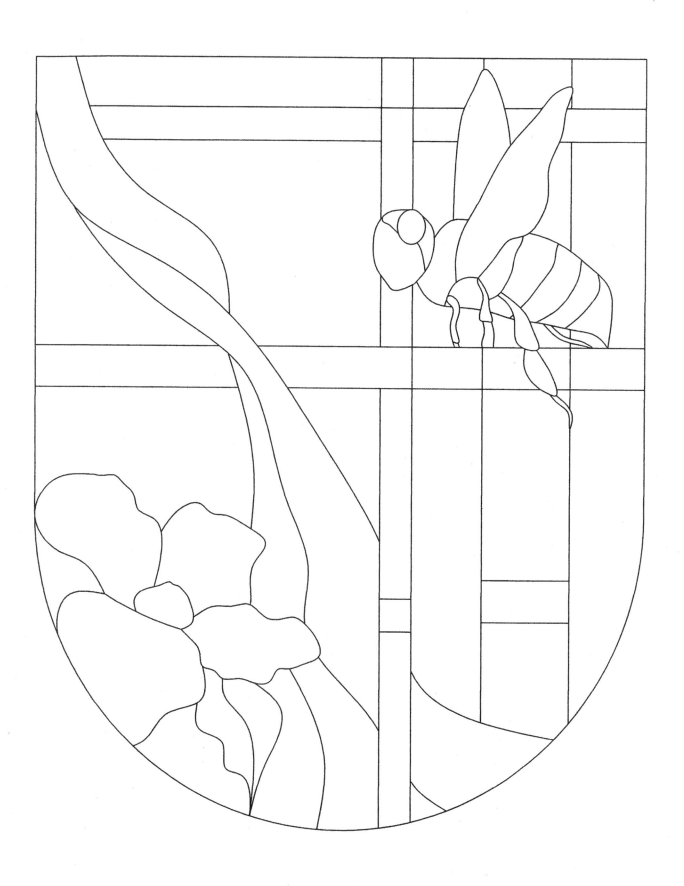

36   WATER LILY

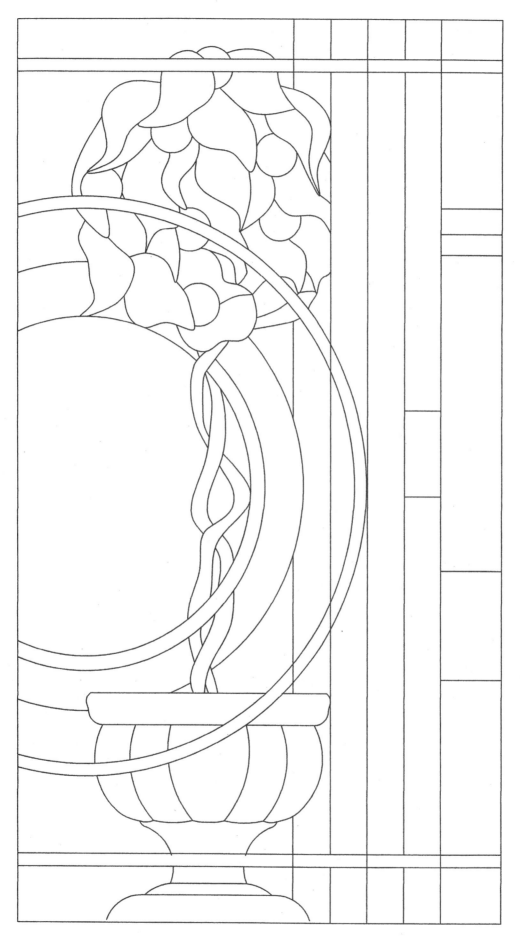

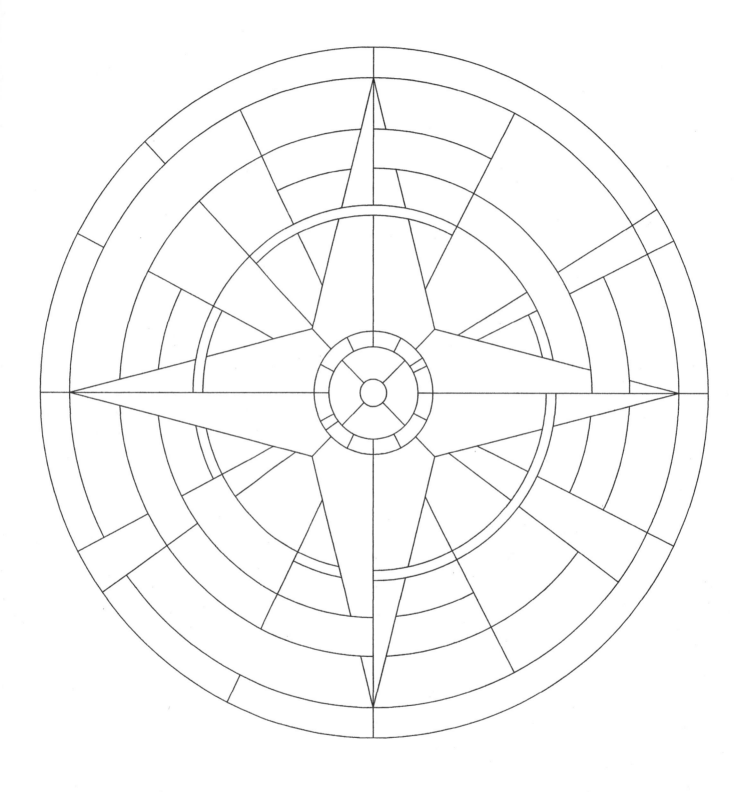

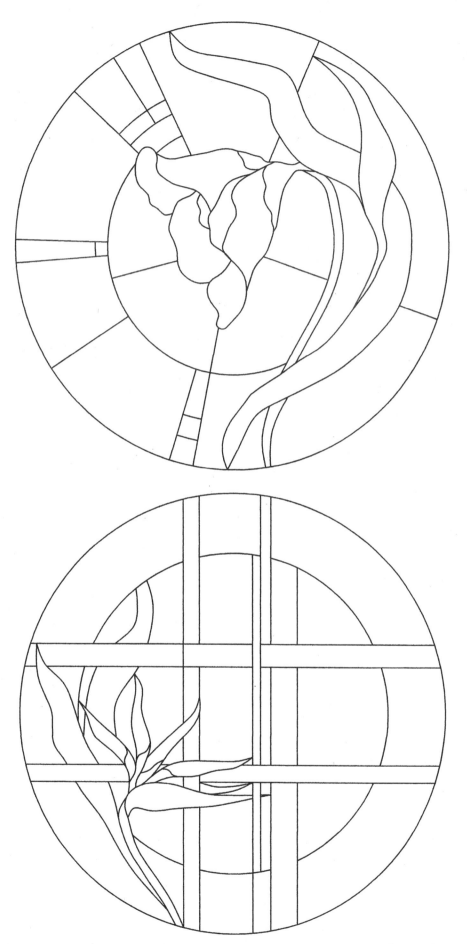

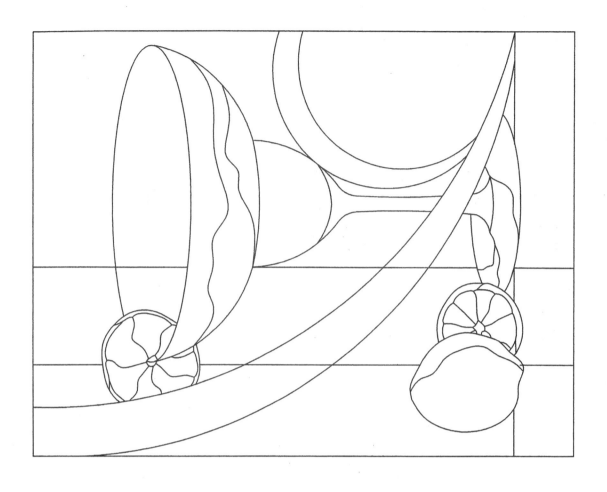

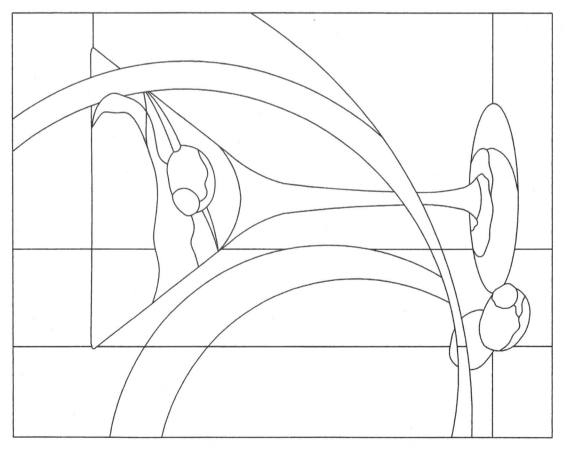

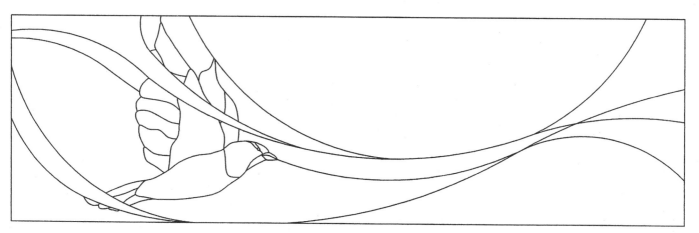

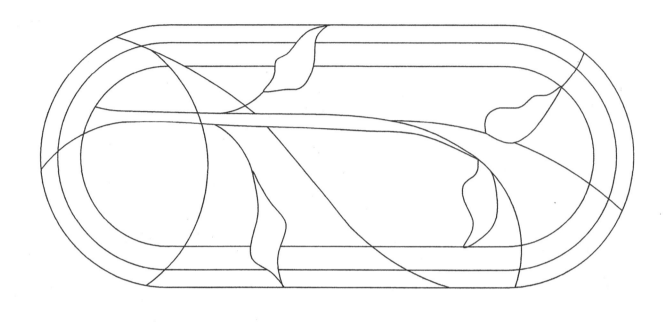

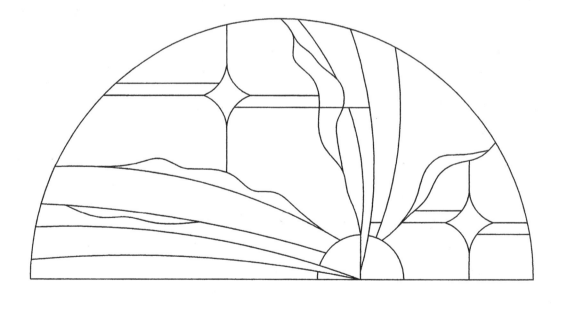

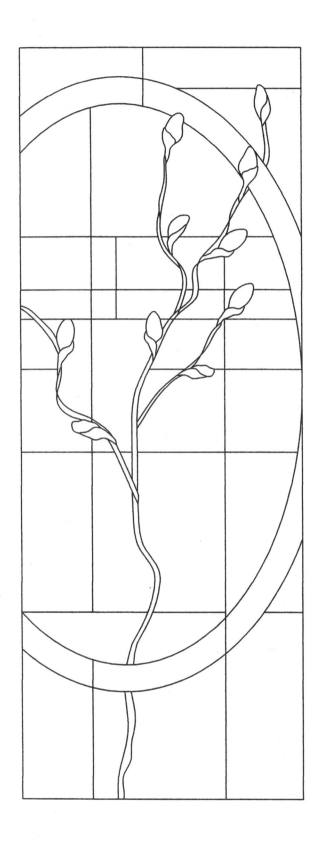

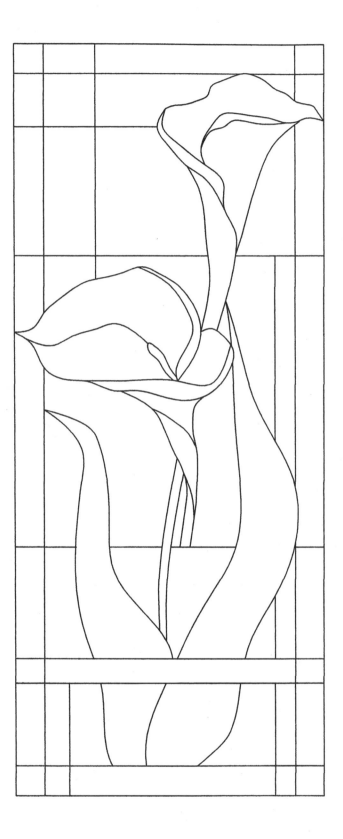

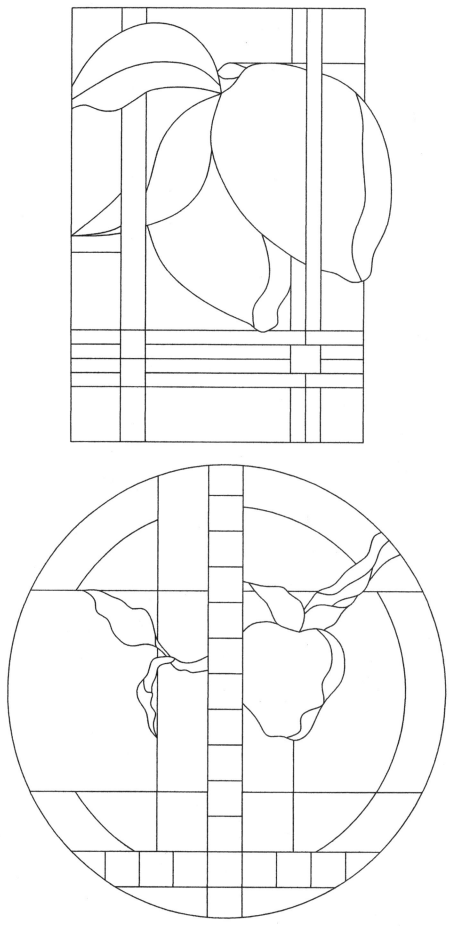

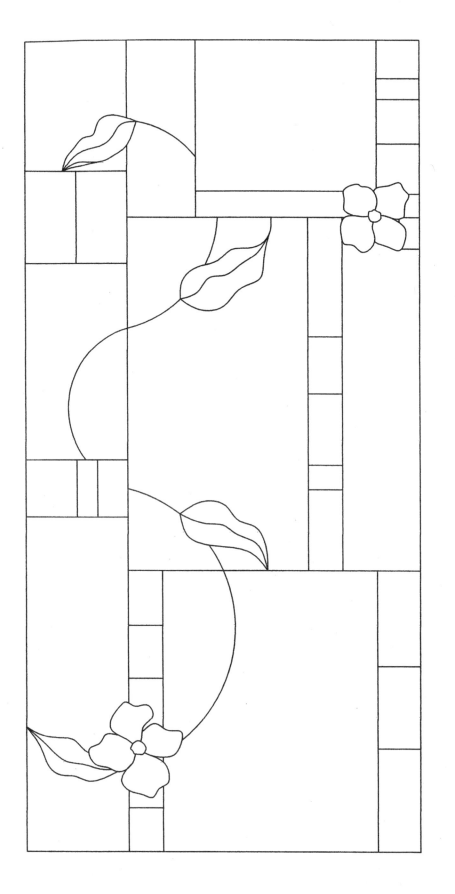
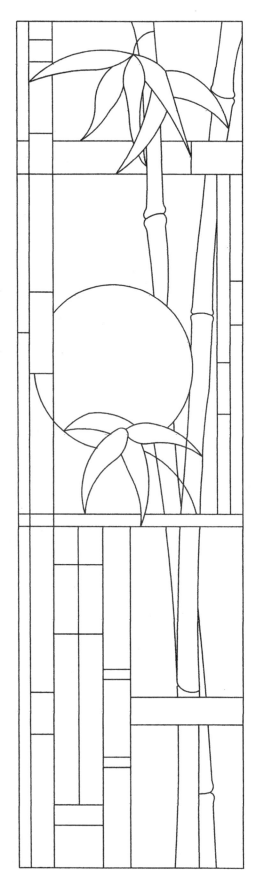

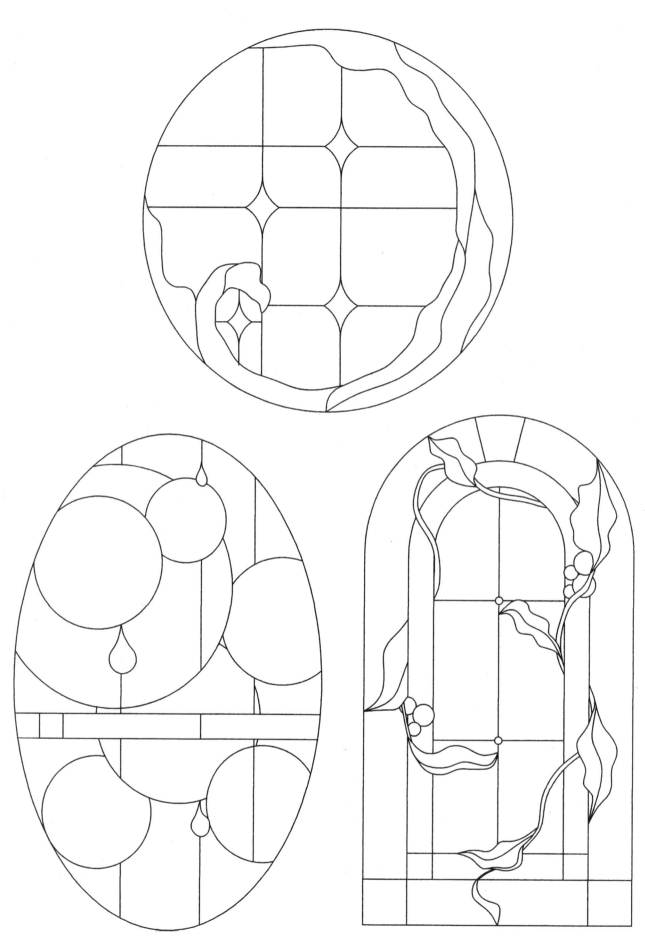

MOON AND STARS; RAINDROPS; VINE

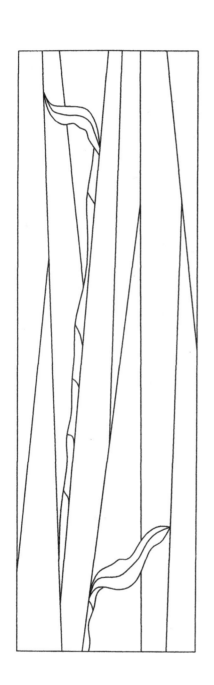

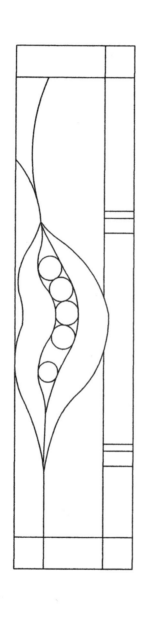

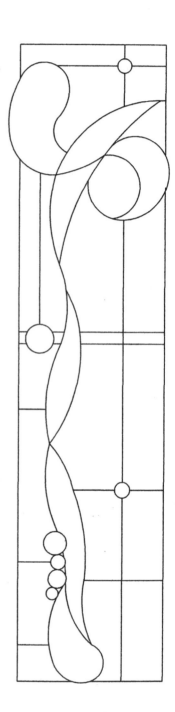

54   BIRCH BRANCH; PEAPOD; WAVE AND BUBBLES

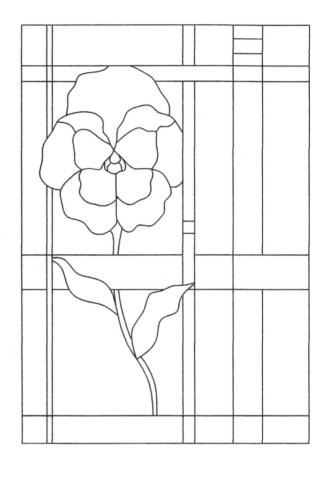

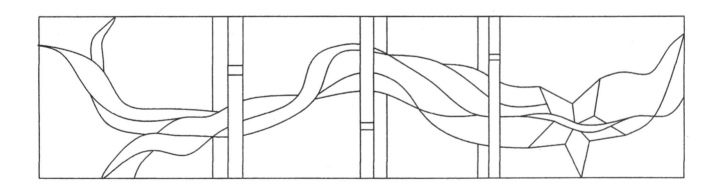

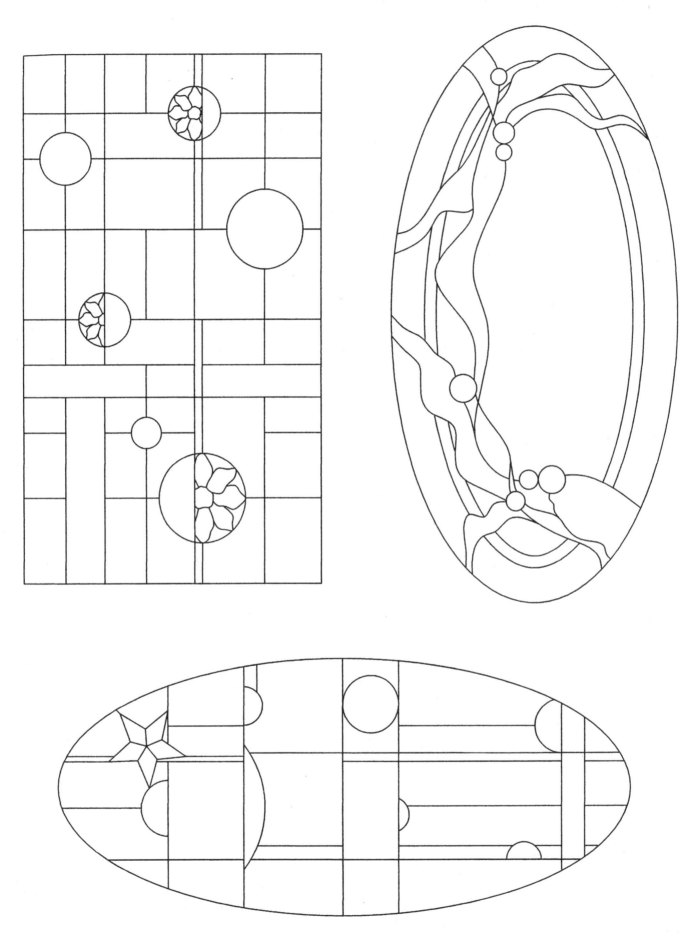

58   DAISIES; WATER AND BUBBLES; STAR AND PLANETS

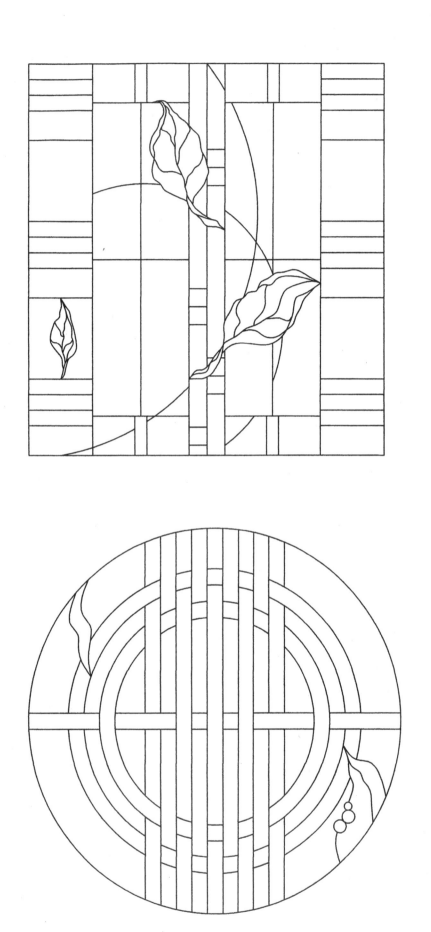

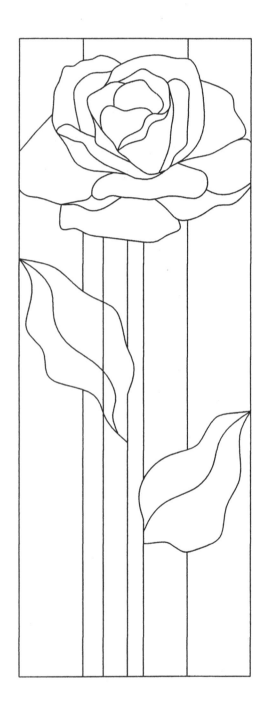

60   ELM LEAVES; ROSE; WATER AND BUBBLES